TRUE STORIES OF

Animal Heroes

BY ARNOLD RINGSTAD

Published by The Child's World®
1980 Lookout Drive • Mankato, MN 56003-1705
800-599-READ • www.childsworld.com

Acknowledgments
The Child's World®: Mary Berendes, Publishing Director
Red Line Editorial: Editorial direction
The Design Lab: Design
Amnet: Production

Photographs © He Zinyong/ICHPL Imaginechina/AP Images,
cover (top), 1 (top), 2–3, 11; Damian Dovarganes/AP Images,
cover (center), 1 (center), 19; Tony Campbell/Thinkstock, cover
(bottom right), 1 (bottom right), 3 (bottom), 17; Alexia
Khruscheva/Shutterstock Images, back cover (top), 3 (top right);
Roman Samokhin/Shutterstock Images, back cover (bottom), 23;
AP Images, 4, 7; PDSA/AP Images, 5, 20; AnetaPics/
Shutterstock Images, 8; Ministry of Defence/AP Images, 9;
Rui Pestana/Thinkstock, 10; Doug Kanter/AP Images, 12–13;
PhotoDisc, 14; Todd Plitt/AP Images, 15; Bettmann/Corbis, 16

ISBN 9781626873582
LCCN 2014930697

Printed in the United States of America
Mankato, MN
July, 2014
PA02225

ABOUT THE AUTHOR

Arnold Ringstad lives in Minnesota. His cat loves stories about feline heroes.

CONTENTS

ANIMAL HEROES

Some animals overcome fear to act heroically. Their bravery is inspiring to people. A bomb-sniffing dog saved a soldier's life. A pigeon helped deliver messages in wars. A gorilla came to the rescue of an **injured** *child. These are just a few examples of brave animals. Read on to learn more about these and other stories of animal heroes.*

This gorilla is just one animal hero.

Saving Lives in London

Dogs can be especially heroic after disasters. They smell and hear very well. Dogs' noses and ears help them find victims buried in **rubble**. One of the first rescue dogs was named Rip. He saved lives in London, England.

During World War II (1939–1945), the city of London was often bombed. The bombs blew up buildings. People got trapped in the rubble. Some bombs did not explode right away. This made them even more dangerous. People looking for survivors could accidentally set them off. At first, human workers searched for victims. But they soon realized dogs could save more lives.

Rip was one of these rescue dogs. People had to train most dogs to search through rubble. But Rip knew how to safely find trapped people. In all, he saved more than 100 lives. He won the Dickin Medal in 1945. This award is given to brave animals that take heroic actions.

Rip was one of the first animals to earn the Dickin Medal.

5

A Lifesaving Gorilla

Gorillas are big, powerful beasts. Some people think gorillas are scary. But this story may change their minds. Jambo the gorilla lived at Jersey Zoo in Europe. He took heroic action that may have saved the life of a young boy.

In 1986, the Merritt family visited the Jersey Zoo. The family's five-year-old boy, Levan, was with them. They stopped at the gorilla enclosure. Levan's father lifted him up to get a better view. Suddenly, Levan climbed over the wall. He fell 12 feet (3.7 m) onto concrete and injured himself. The gorillas walked toward him. Zoo visitors feared the worst.

Then, something unexpected happened. Jambo stood between Levan and the other gorillas. He stopped them from getting close to Levan. Soon, zookeepers moved the gorillas into their cages. Rescuers entered the gorilla area. They got Levan out. They took him to the hospital. He ended up healing and being just fine. The story amazed people around the world. People nicknamed Jambo "the Gentle Giant."

Jambo sits near injured Levan.

A Dog at War

Some of the biggest dangers in the Afghanistan War (2001–) are bombs on roads. The bombs can blow up trucks and injure people. The British military found a way to find the bombs before they blew up. The military used dogs to search for the bombs. Dogs have a powerful sense of smell. The dogs easily sniffed out the buried bombs. Then, the bombs could be safely destroyed. People would not be harmed.

Military dogs use their noses to sniff out bombs.

One brave, bomb-sniffing dog was named Theo. He worked with Lance Corporal (LCpl.) Liam Tasker. LCpl. Tasker was a British soldier in Afghanistan. Theo helped him find 14 bombs in just five months.

LCpl. Tasker and Theo train in Afghanistan.

That was more than any other dog in Afghanistan.

Theo and LCpl. Tasker helped save many lives by finding bombs. Theo even won the Dickin Medal for his brave actions.

A Pig Survivor

Not all animal heroes save lives. Some inspire people with their incredible stories of survival. You might not think a pig could be a heroic animal. But a pig named Zhu Jianqiang inspired people across the world.

Zhu lived in China. In 2008, a strong earthquake struck the area where he lived. The earthquake shook buildings.

A powerful earthquake caused this destruction in China.

Zhu relaxes after his rescue.

It knocked many of them over. Tens of thousands of people were killed. Zhu was in his **sty** when the earthquake hit. Amazingly, the 330-pound (150 kg) pig lived through it. But his survival adventure was just beginning.

Zhu was buried in the rubble for 36 days. People were amazed when they found him alive. Zhu was injured, but he was okay. The brave pig survived by eating charcoal and drinking rainwater. Chinese newspapers called Zhu a national hero.

Apollo the Rescue Dog

On September 11, 2001, there was a terrible attack on New York City. It caused two huge buildings to fall down. They were

called the World Trade Center towers. Firefighters and police officers spent days looking for survivors in the rubble. Specially trained dogs helped them. One of the dogs was named Apollo.

Apollo and his handler, Pete Davis, searched the area. They arrived less than an hour after the buildings fell. Their work was very dangerous. Smoke and fire surrounded them. The rubble was unstable. A burning piece of building fell down around Apollo. He almost got badly injured. That did not stop Apollo, though. He got up and continued to search for survivors. Apollo won the Dickin Medal for his bravery.

Apollo and his handler Pete Davis worked for the New York City Police Department.

A Fiery Rescue

In 1996, an incredible animal rescue caught the world's attention. It happened in a garage in Brooklyn, New York. The garage was **abandoned**. No people were using it. Instead, a cat named Scarlet lived there with her five kittens. One day, a fire broke out in the garage. The cats were still inside. Someone in the neighborhood noticed. The fire department came right away.

FUN FACT

A group that protects animals named a new award after Scarlet. The award is given to animal heroes.

The firefighters saw an amazing sight. Scarlet was carrying her kittens out of the garage one by one. Though she was badly burned, Scarlet rescued all of her kittens.

The cats were brought to an animal **shelter.** They soon became world famous. They appeared on television shows across the globe. Three months after the rescue, the cats were finally healthy. Karen Wellen of Brooklyn adopted Scarlet. Wellen said, "She was the most precious and loving cat in our household."

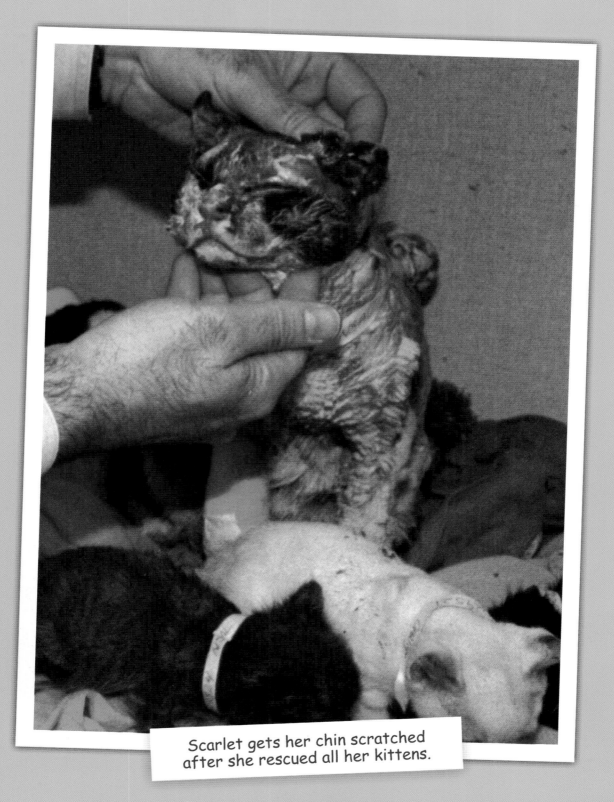

Scarlet gets her chin scratched after she rescued all her kittens.

A Horse on the Front Lines

Sergeant Reckless eats cake at a dinner where she was the guest of honor.

The Korean War was fought between 1950 and 1953.
U.S. soldiers experienced cold weather and rocky mountains.
They sometimes suffered from low supplies. Heroic animals

carried supplies from place to place. One of them was a horse named Reckless.

U.S. soldier Eric Pederson bought Reckless from a young boy in Seoul, Korea. He paid $250 for her. The horse carried bullets to soldiers on the front lines. She returned with wounded soldiers on her back. Reckless bravely ran through dangerous areas. Bullets and bombs flew around her. But Reckless kept delivering bullets. In one battle alone, she made 51 trips to the front lines.

The U.S. military promoted Reckless to the rank of Staff Sergeant. They gave her many awards for her service. She especially loved the food rewards soldiers gave her, though. Sergeant Reckless liked to eat chocolate and pancakes. She even drank soda!

Reckless was awarded a Purple Heart during the Korean War.

A Heroic Pit Bull

Some people think pit bulls are mean dogs. They are sometimes in the news for biting people. But most pit bulls are friendly. One pit bull from California was even a hero. Her name was Diamond.

Diamond lived with the Steen family in Hayward, California. Darryl Steen lived in an apartment with his two daughters. One night, the family was sleeping when their apartment caught fire. Diamond noticed the fire and barked. She woke the family up. Darryl brought his 9-year-old daughter to safety. But his 16-year-old daughter was missing. Diamond quickly found the missing girl hiding under a bed. Diamond protected the girl from the flames until firefighters arrived.

Diamond was badly burned. She had to visit a **veterinarian**. The bill was more than $5,000. Word got out about Diamond's amazing rescue. People donated more than enough money to pay the bill. Darryl said, "[Diamond] means everything to me. If it hadn't been for this dog, me and my girls wouldn't be alive."

Diamond suffered some burns
during her heroic actions.

War Pigeon

Pigeons are unlikely animal heroes. Some people who live in big cities think these birds are annoying. But pigeons were once respected heroes. Militaries used them to deliver messages during wars. The birds are naturally good at

Winkie is presented with her Dickin Medal.

finding their way back home. This made them useful for carrying messages during wartime. Sometimes, they even saved lives. Winkie the pigeon was one of these lifesaving birds.

During World War II (1939–1945), a British airplane was shot down in the ocean. Four crew members were aboard. They were far from land. Rescue seemed impossible. However, they had a carrier pigeon named Winkie. They released her, and she flew away. They hoped Winkie would fly back home to the United Kingdom.

Winkie reached her home on a British military **base**. Soldiers at the base realized what had happened. They sent a rescue mission to find the airplane crew. The men were rescued in only 15 minutes. It was all thanks to the brave pigeon. Winkie became the first animal to win the Dickin Medal.

FUN FACT
People once sent messages on pigeons by tying tiny little notes to the birds' legs. The United Kingdom used about 250,000 of these birds during World War II (1939–1945).

abandoned (uh-BAN-dund) When something is abandoned, it is left empty and unused. Scarlet and her kittens lived in an abandoned garage.

base (base) A base is a place where soldiers work. Winkie the pigeon flew back to a military base.

injured (IN-jurd) If something is injured, it is damaged or harmed. Many animals become injured as a result of their heroic actions.

rubble (RUB-ul) Rubble is pieces of a building left after it falls down. Dogs are trained to find survivors underneath rubble.

shelter (SHEL-tur) A shelter is a place where people take care of animals without homes. The injured cats were taken to a shelter.

sty (sty) A sty is a building where pigs live. Zhu the pig's sty fell down in an earthquake.

veterinarian (VET-ur-eh-NAIR-ee-un) A veterinarian is a doctor who takes care of animals. A veterinarian treated Diamond the dog's burns.

TO LEARN MORE

BOOKS

125 True Stories of Amazing Animals: Inspiring Tales of Animal Friendship and Four-Legged Heroes, Plus Crazy Animal Antics. Washington, DC: National Geographic, 2012.

Halls, Kelly Milner. *Courageous Canine: And More True Stories of Amazing Animal Heroes.* Washington, DC: National Geographic, 2013.

Markle, Sandra. *Animal Heroes: True Rescue Stories.* Minneapolis, MN: Millbrook, 2009.

WEB SITES

Visit our Web site for links about animal heroes: *childsworld.com/links*

Note to Parents, Teachers, and Librarians:
We routinely verify our Web links to make sure they are safe and active sites. So encourage your readers to check them out!